A Good Ride

by Andrea Patel
illustrated by Tom Leonard

Core Decodable 94

Bothell, WA • Chicago, IL • Columbus, OH • New York, NY

MHEonline.com

McGraw Hill Education

Copyright © 2015 McGraw-Hill Education

All rights reserved. No part of this publication may be reproduced or distributed in any form or by any means, or stored in a database or retrieval system, without the prior written consent of McGraw-Hill Education, including, but not limited to, network storage or transmission, or broadcast for distance learning.

Send all inquiries to:
McGraw-Hill Education
8787 Orion Place
Columbus, OH 43240

ISBN: 978-0-02-132282-4
MHID: 0-02-132282-1

Printed in the United States of America.

2 3 4 5 6 7 8 9 DOC 20 19 18 17 16 15

A bug jumped on a leaf in a brook.
"Now I will take a ride," she said.

The bug had a foot in the brook.
She looked ahead.

The brook was now a quick stream.
"This is a good ride," said the bug.
She stood up.

The stream took a sharp turn.
Now it was a fast river.
The leaf shook.

Look at the high falls!
"I am afraid," the bug called.
Now she shook and shook.

The bug rode down the falls!
"I took a good ride!" she said.